Our beautiful Earth has 7 continents. Each continent encompasses different contries.

In this fun book, You, LITTLE EPLORER, will Travel With Us in each one of those adorable continents. You will get to know them more and you will explore differents contries . ENJOY

NORTH AMERICA

North America is a continent which is located entirely on the northern and western hemisphere. It includes 23 countries :Canada, Mexico, the United States of America (USA), the Caribbean islands and various other countries.

CANADA

The capital city of Canada is Ottawa. Canada is the second largest contry in the world by total area. Two languages are mainly spoken in Canada: Frensh and English. Winter is very cold in Canada. Temperature drops below −40 °C in some parts of the country.

THE UNITED STATES OF AMERICA (USA)

The USA IS is the third largest country in the world. The capital city of the USA is called Washington D.C. D.C. stands for District of Columbia. Largest city in the USA is New York. The USA shares land borders with Canada and with Mexico. The national flag of the USA has 13 stripes and 50 white stars on blue background.

MEXICO

The capital city of Canada is .
Mexico city. Mexicans speak spanish.
Mexico was conquered and colonised
by the Spanish from the 16th century.
Mexico
has mountains in its east and north,
rainforests in its south, and deserts
in the West.

SOUTH AMERICA

SOUTH AMERICA IS THE FOURTH LARGEST CONTINENT IN SIZE AND THE FIFTH LARGEST WHEN WE CONSIDER POPULATION. THE CONTINENT IS LOCATED IN THE WESTERN HEMISPHERE AND MAINLY IN THE SOUTHERN HEMISPHERE. SOUTH AMERICA INCLUDES 12 COUNTRIES.

BRAZIL

The capital city of Brazil is Brasilia. Sao Paulo is the largest city in the country by total area. The habitants speak Portuguese. Brazil also belongs to the Latin American countries.
The country borders the Atlantic Ocean..

ARGENTINA

Argentina is the world's eight largest country and second largest country in South America after Brazil. 45.5 million people live in Argentina. Its capital is Buenos Aires. Argentina covers about one third as much land area compared with the size of the USA.

CHILE

The republic of chile shares borders with the Pacific Ocean and the three South American countries: Peru, Bolivia and Argentina. Chile is home to the world's largest dry desert: the Atacama desert. The capital city of Chile is Santiago.

AFRICA

Africa covers over 30 million square kilometres, is bigger than the USA, Canada and India together. About 2000 different languages are spoken on the African continent. There are 54 countries in Africa.

ALGERIA

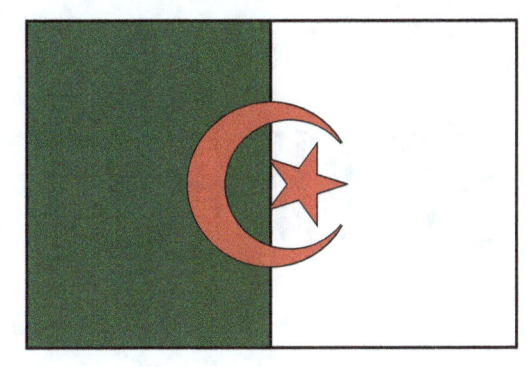

Algeria is a country in the Western part of North Africa. The capital city is Algiers. It is the largest country in Africa. The country borders the Atlantic Ocean. A large part of southern Algeria is the Sahara Desert. Official languages are Arabic, Berber and French.

SOUTH AFRICA

South Africa is the southernmost country on the African continent. It has various mountain ranges and the grasslands. South african safari is full of jungle animals
like monkeys, lions, tigers...
Pretoria is the capital city. There are 11 offical languages in South Africa.

MOROCCO

The kingdom of Morocco is Morocco is located in the northwest corner of Africa and is bordered by the North Atlantic Ocean and the Mediterranean Sea.
Moroccans are know by their hospitality and their delecious food. The capital city is Rabat. Moroccans are Berber and Arab and most of the people are Muslim

EGYPT

Egypt's capital is Cairo. Without the Nile River, all of Egypt would be desert. Only about an inch of rain falls throughout Egypt each year. Egypt is home to a wide variety of animals and plants, including jackals, gazelles, crocodiles, and cobras. Huge pyramids are build in Egypt.

AUSTRALIA

Australia, called also Oceania is the smallest continent of the seven continents. Australia is commonly referred to as a country and a continent.
Australia is also the driest inhabited continent of the world.

AUSTRALIA

Australia is an island country. It is the sixth largest country in the world, The capital city is Canberra. The biggest city in Australia is Sydney. The official language is english. Australia is home to many animal species: Kangaroo, Koala...

ASIA

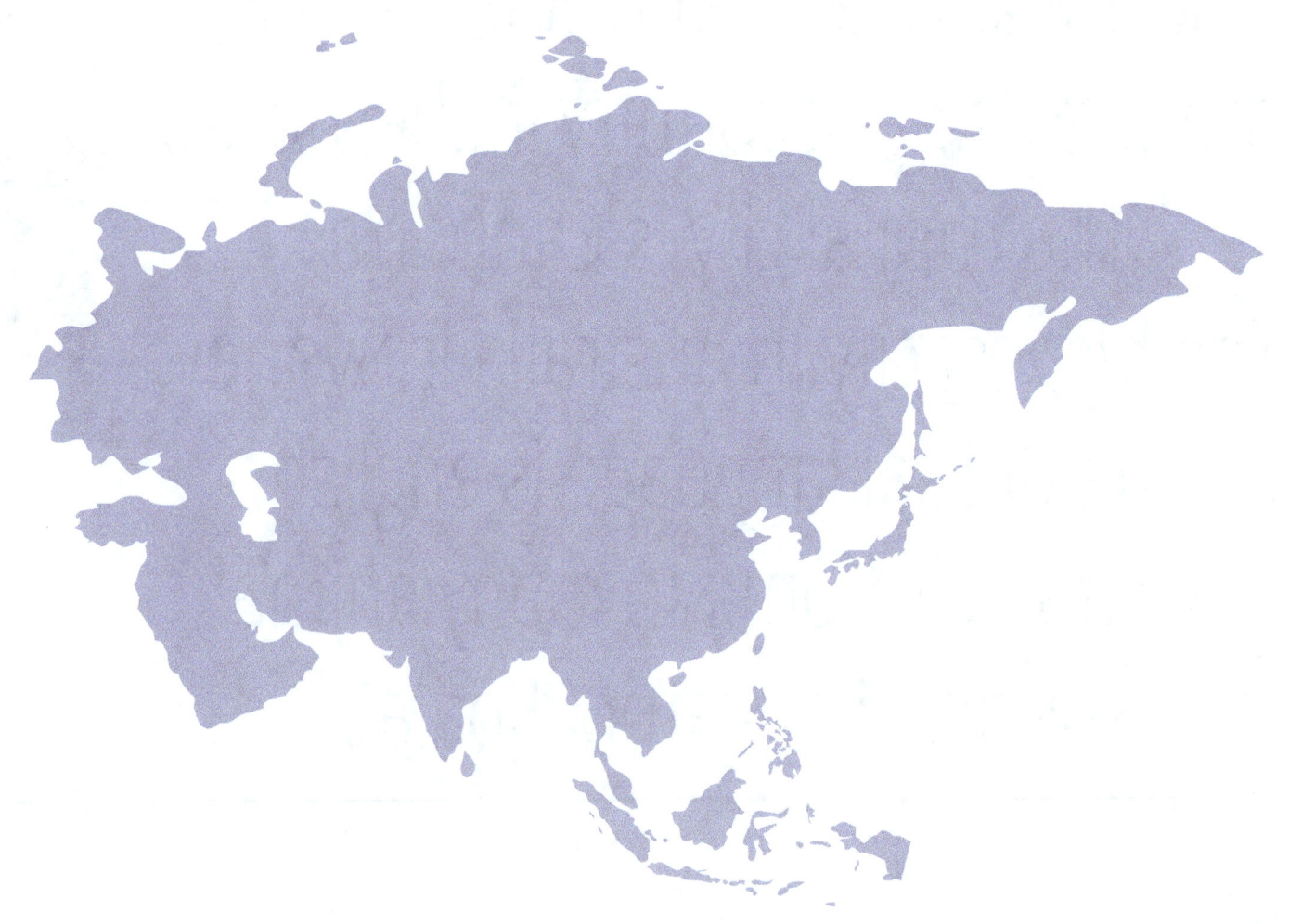

Asia is the largest continent of our planet, with the most people living on it.

The Asian continent includes 48 countries. In Asia more than 2,300 languages are recognised.

It contains also the world's highest peak Mount Everest.

JAPAN

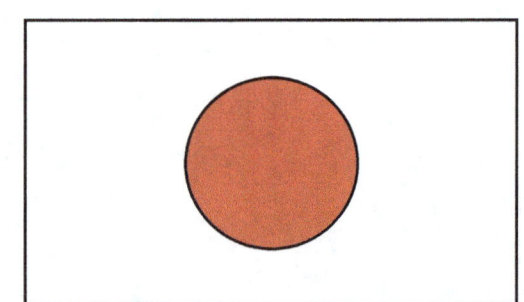

Japan is is a chain of islands.
Its capital is Tokyo, which is the biggest city in the country.
Japanese is the official language.
Japan is the oldest monarchy in the world and has an emperor.

RUSSIA

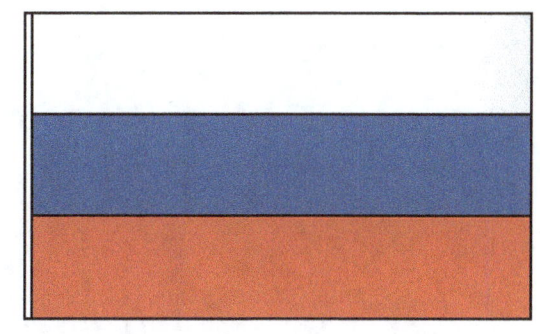

Russia is the world's largest country. it is a huge country that is double the size of Australia. The capital city is Moscow, which is Russia's largest city. Almost half of the country is covered in forests.

CHINA

China is the second largest country in Asia and the fourth in the world. China borders 14 countries. China is the most populous country. The capital city is Beijing.

INDIA

New Delhi is the capital city of India. This country is the second most populous in the world. It has 22 official languages. India borders seven 7 countries, China is one of them. India is also known for its food, mostly for curry.

EUROPE

Europe is the second smallest continent in Earth. It contains 46 countries.
It is bordered by the Mediterranean Sea to the south, Asia to the east, and the Atlantic Ocean to the West.

FRANCE

The capital city of France is Paris, called the city of love. French is the official language in France and it is also the second major language in Europe. Many tourists visit France to enjoy its attractions like Eiffel Tower.

ITALY

Italy is one of the fewest countries that have a long history. Its capital is Roma. It borders six countries. Italien food is so rich and also known all over the world. Pizza, Pasta, Gelato are Italien inventions.

UNITED KINGDOM

The United Kingdom or UK is a group of united islands in Europe. It is made up of four parts: England, Scotland, Wales, and Northern Ireland . The capital city is London. We call United Kingdom's habitant British.

ANTARCTICA

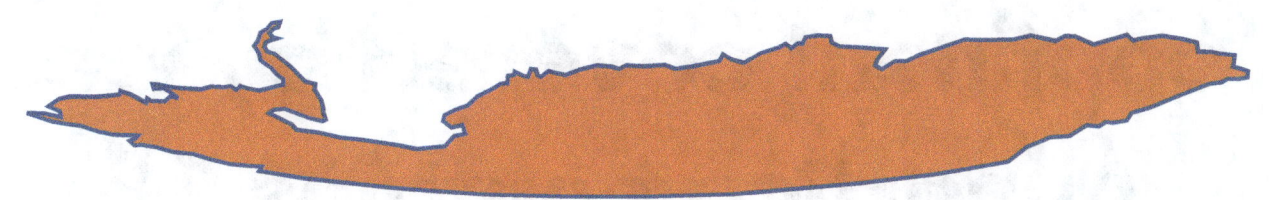

Antarctica is the least populated continent of our planet. It is a continent covered by ice. Ancartica contains 18 countries. Penguins are the only animal existing on Antarctica.

Copyright 2022 by My Stars Books
All Rights Reserved

No part of this book may be produced or transmitted in any form by any means whatsoever without express written permission from the author, except in the case of brief quotations embodied in critical articles and reviews.

Please refer all pertinent questions to the publisher.

My Stars Books
THE SHELF WITH BEAUTIFUL STORIES

/MyStarsBooks   /MyStarsBooks

Thank you for your recent purchase.

Positive feedback from our valued customers really helps us to continue attracting more great customers such as yourself and to improve our work.
If you wouldn't mind leaving an online review section, we would really appreciate that.

www.ingramcontent.com/pod-product-compliance
Lightning Source LLC
Chambersburg PA
CBHW081628100526
44590CB00021B/3657